WIZARD OF THE GREAT LAKE

WIZARD OF THE GREAT LAKE

The Story of Alexander Mackay

by
DONALD McFARLAN

CHRISTIAN LITERATURE CRUSADE
FORT WASHINGTON   PENNSYLVANIA 19034

CHRISTIAN LITERATURE CRUSADE

Fort Washington, Pennsylvania 19034

First paperback edition 1975

PRINTED IN GREAT BRITAIN

CONTENTS

1

THE YOUNG ENGINEER

THE small boy gazed critically at the map which hung from the bookcase in a corner of the study.

"Africa must be a very empty place," he said. "Only a few rivers and mountains. Where do the black people live? Are there no towns and roads anywhere?"

His father smiled. "Come over here, Alec," he said. "You see that river there?" He pointed to a wandering black line on the map. "That's the mighty Niger. It was discovered by one of our own countrymen, Mungo Park. Many, many tribes live along its banks."

His forefinger traced the line of another river on the east of the continent. "And there's the Zambesi, David Livingstone's river."

Alexander Mackay nodded. "That's where the Victoria Falls are," he said. David Livingstone was the hero of every Scottish boy, and he had often listened eagerly while his father read bits from the newspapers about the travels of the famous missionary explorer.

"But where are the towns and the roads?" he insisted.

"The towns aren't marked on the map yet," was the reply. "I suppose only Doctor Livingstone and pioneers like him know just where the people live. As for roads, there just aren't any. Not proper highways, anyway. Only tracks through the forest, and the paths followed by the slave-traders."

The boy listened thoughtfully while his father described David Livingstone's encounter with the Arab slavers who drove their wretched captives like cattle to the coast.

"Maybe some day there will be roads all over Africa," he said. "Then people will be able to travel easily without being attacked by wild beasts and wild men."

"I hope so," agreed his father. "What Africa needs is men to open up peaceful roads, like the one in the Bible: 'A highway shall be there, and a way, and it shall be called the way of holiness; . . . no lion shall be there, nor any ravenous beast shall go thereon, it shall not be found there; but the redeemed shall walk there. . . .' "

Dr. Mackay lifted the map down from the book-case and put it in his son's hands.

"You're quite right, there are still a lot of empty spaces to be filled in," he said. "But every year the newspapers and magazines are telling us more about the discoveries of the explorers. You are neat with your hands, Alec, I've noticed that. You take the map and keep it up to date. I have filled in most of the features of Africa I have read about, but there will be plenty more to put in during the coming years."

The boy's eyes shone with delight. "I'll be careful, father," he promised. "No blots or mistakes. Only, you must help me to draw the rivers and mountains in their right place."

His father spread the map on the table by the window. "We can put something in this very day," he said. "Get your pen, my lad, and make sure there's no hair in the nib."

He guided his son's hand over the paper. "There," he said, pointing to a spot just on the equator. "Draw a lake, Alec."

The boy hesitated. "How big?" he asked.

His father scratched his head. "That's a question!" he said. "I don't suppose anyone knows the answer to that yet. But we do know that it's a big lake, far, far bigger than any of our Scottish lochs, for example."

He watched his son make a bold outline on the map. "That's well done," he approved. "Now put in the name: Lake Victoria Nyanza."

Alexander carefully inked in the words, stopping only to ask the spelling of the African name.

"It was discovered only this year, by the traveller John Hanning Speke," his father went on. "For all we know, it is the biggest lake in the whole of Africa."

*   *   *

To young Alexander Mackay the map of Africa

became the main point of interest in his father's study. The year was 1858, and he was nine years old. His father was Free Church minister in the little village of Rhynie, in Aberdeenshire. Alexander had never been to school, but that did not mean that he was idle and ignorant. On the contrary, he had already read more than most boys of his age. The Reverend Dr. Mackay, like many another country minister of his time, was a scholar as well as a pastor, and he had been his son's teacher from the time the boy could listen and learn. The cosy manse study was Alexander's school room and the volumes which lined the walls were his reading-books.

When he was only three years old he was reading the New Testament, and by the time he was seven he knew the contents of many of the history books on his father's shelves. There were no "comics" in those days, or easily-read children's books. Alexander had to battle with the big words and long paragraphs of *The Decline and Fall of the Roman Empire* and such-like tomes. But he and his father had the delight of talking everything over together, not only in the study, but during the long walks they took about the countryside.

The village folk used to wonder what their minister was doing when they saw him stop so often on the road, talking earnestly all the time to the boy by his side.

"See here, Alec," he would say, drawing in the

dust with his stick. "These angles are equal, and so the sides are equal, too. That's geometry, and it's always true, whether you're in Scotland, or China, or darkest Africa. If ever you've to measure a bit of land, you'll find that useful."

A little later they would stop again to have a look at an age-old fossil, or to draw another diagram in the road to show the motion of the stars. Thus young Alexander gained a great deal of information about all sorts of subjects, and what he learned he remembered.

As he grew older, his special interest was in machinery. He thought nothing of walking four miles to the nearest railway station to have a good look at the hissing engine as it stopped for a few minutes on its way to the north. Books were almost neglected now. He spent hours at the village smithy, helping the blacksmith to blow the bellows and watching him shape the glowing iron into sturdy implements for field and farm.

At home, during the long winter evenings, his favourite hobby was printing, with the aid of a small printing-press his father had brought him from Edinburgh. As Dr. Mackay had said, he was neat with his hands, "knacky", as the Scots called it, and anything that "worked" was his delight. But he did not forget his map of Africa. Hour after hour was spent carefully tracing on it the results of explorations he had read about in the newspapers. Lake Victoria Nyanza was no longer an isolated circle somewhere in the heart of the Dark Continent. The explorer Speke had reported it to be the long-sought source of the Nile. Furthermore, he had declared that Uganda, the vast territory which lay along the north-west of the lake, was a land desperately in need of missionaries.

*   *   *

When he was fourteen, Alexander was sent to the Grammar School in Aberdeen. His parents hoped that he would one day be a minister like his father, and for that he must return to his books. Study he did, but all his spare time in the granite city was spent in one of the shipbuilding yards down by the harbour.

There was a solemn interview in the manse study when he came home for the holidays. Dr. Mackay studied his son's school report card.

"You're doing well, Alec," he said. "I see you are top in Latin, Greek and Mathematics. I've no complaint about that."

He looked at his son over the top of his spectacles.

"But I've a letter here from my friend Mr. Ferguson," he went on more sternly. "He tells me that you never seem to have time to join their family on Saturdays. I want a frank answer, Alec. What have you been doing with yourself?"

Alexander Mackay swallowed hard. Then the words came with a rush.

"I've been down at the yards, father, the ship-yards, I mean. Sometimes the engineers let me give a hand. They're building a ship just now with the very latest thing in engines. I've got a drawing of it here that I copied myself. See, I'll show you!" He tugged a large sheet of paper from his satchel.

Dr. Mackay shook his head. "You're wasting far too much time on these childish hobbies, my boy. You must stick into your books, or you'll never be a minister."

Alexander's blue eyes challenged his father. "I'm sorry, father," he said quietly. "But I've made up my mind. I'm not going to be a minister. I want to be an engineer!"

*   *   *

The next few years saw him steadily pursuing his resolve. At Edinburgh University he applied himself to all the mysteries of mechanics and engineering, higher mathematics and surveying. In the afternoons, when classes were done for the day, he donned overalls and toiled in a local engineering works, learning with his hands as well as with his head. On Sundays he was a Sunday School teacher in the slums of Edinburgh. But in spite of his busy life, Alexander Mackay was later to wish that he had packed even more into his student days. In a letter to his father from Africa he was to write:

"I only wish I had got double the amount of

education, not only in the way of book-learning, but also in practical skill. No man can know enough, and be able to turn his hand to too many things, to be a useful missionary in Central Africa."

His apprenticeship finished, Mackay went on to Germany to learn still more about engineering. He got a post as draughtsman in a large locomotive works in Berlin. His boyhood interest in railway engines, in anything that "worked", found full expression in the designing of many different kinds of machinery. There was a proud moment when he won first prize for an agricultural machine of his own invention at an exhibition in Breslau.

But he never forgot Africa. Eagerly he read in the British newspapers which his sister posted to him about the opening up of the Dark Continent, and the need for missionaries. He wrote to her:

"I am not a doctor, and therefore cannot go as such; but I am an engineer, and propose, if the Lord will, to go as an engineering missionary. Of course I am as yet far from prepared to undertake such a task, especially alone; and of course many obstacles stand in the way. You will ask how am I to get there. You will ask what am I to do when I get there. Well, I hope especially to connect Christianity with modern civilization. I expect to execute public works, as railways, mines, etc., which, for one single-handed, is an enormous enterprise. It is more to help the missionaries that are there already that I go, than to supplant them;

also to prepare the way by which others more readily can go there and stay."

But was there a post for an engineer missionary? Mackay was convinced that there was, but he met with one disappointment after another. He heard of the call for missionaries for Madagascar and wrote to offer his services there. But the reply was that his help was not needed at that time. Nothing daunted, he went on with his daily work, spending all his spare time in the study of Malagasy, the language of Madagascar.

Six months later he read an appeal from the Church Missionary Society for a layman to take over the supervision of a settlement for liberated slaves near Mombasa. A practical man was needed, one who could erect buildings, make roads, and serve as a competent engineer. Mackay's heart leaped as he read these words. Surely this was his call? He reached for his pen.

But again there was disappointment. The reply to his offer of service was that the C.M.S. had already found a man for the post.

Was the door closed against his desire to be a missionary? It seemed so. Meanwhile a tempting offer of promotion came his way. The chief director of the German engineering firm had noted the young Scotsman's ability, and he proposed to make him a partner in a similar firm which was being opened in Moscow. Fortune and fame lay before him.

But Mackay's heart was set on Africa, and at last the call came. On November 15, 1875, a letter appeared in the columns of the *Daily Telegraph*. It was from H. M. Stanley, the famous explorer who had found Livingstone, and it told of the needs of the ancient kingdom of Uganda.

"Here, gentlemen, is your opportunity," it concluded. "Embrace it! The people on the shores of the Nyanza call upon you."

Stanley's letter was a clarion call to England. Three days after it appeared in the newspaper, the Church Missionary Society had received offers of thousands of pounds to enable them to send missionaries to Uganda. In a short time they had in their hands, too, a letter from Berlin.

"My heart burns for the deliverance of Africa," wrote Alexander Mackay, "and if you send me to any of those regions which Livingstone and Stanley have found to be groaning under the curse of the slave-hunter, I shall be very glad."

This time the answer was Yes! At the age of twenty-six Mackay was appointed along with seven others to be a pioneer of the Gospel in the land of which he had first heard in the quiet country manse of his boyhood days. He was to see the vast lake, the Nyanza, not just a shape which he had inked on the map of Africa, but in its rippling reality.

*　　*　　*

He was frantically busy in the weeks before the

expedition sailed. An engine was to be taken out in sections to be built into a boat for sailing the lake. Mackay worked day and night on the design and stood by while the boiler and other parts were constructed to his satisfaction. He searched London for all kinds of tools which would be essential in a land where he would have to be his own designer, constructor and repairer. Every hour was precious in storing his mind and note-books with practical information about astronomy, printing, iron-puddling, coal-mining, medicine. There was no time even to take a last holiday with his family in Edinburgh.

On April 25, 1876, the committee of the C.M.S. bade farewell to the Uganda Expedition and commended them in prayer to God. Each of the missionaries said a few words, the last speaker being the youngest of the party, Alexander Mackay. There was a stillness in the room as the erect young Scot spoke:

"There is one thing," he said, "which my brethren have not said, and which I want to say. I want to remind the committee that within six months they will probably hear that one of us is dead."

All eyes were fastened on him as he went on: "Yes, is it at all likely that eight Englishmen should start for Central Africa and all be alive six months after? One of us at least—it may be I— will surely fall before that. But when the news

17

comes, do not be cast down, but send someone else immediately to take the vacant place."

Two days later the little company sailed in S. S. *Peshawur* from Southampton. Safely stowed below the decks were the sections of the steam-launch *Daisy* which the young engineer missionary was to put together for voyaging across the uncharted deeps of Lake Victoria Nyanza.

2

THE MAKING OF THE ROAD

ALEXANDER Mackay had little time to admire the scenery as the *Daisy* chugged her way up the River Wami. He was proud of his launch, but there were times when she seemed a fiery dragon calling remorselessly for food. He was the slave of the engine. The African stokers fed the boiler fire almost without a pause, so fiercely did the flames devour cord after cord of firewood. The smoke-stack spat out glowing cinders, the needle quivered on the steam-gauge as the engineer adjusted the throttle, and the launch trembled to the thrust of the propeller. Mackay pushed his sun-helmet back and reached for a sweat-rag to mop his streaming face. So this was Africa!

But he was happy. They were on the move at last, after weeks of enforced idleness on the long voyage to Zanzibar. Their orders were to get past the coastal swamps and make for the Highlands of Africa with all possible speed. Since there were no roads, they were to seek a waterway to the interior. In charge was Lieutenant Smith, late of the Royal Navy, and leader of the missionary expedition. Mackay was engineer, responsible for keeping the launch going at all costs.

For eight days the *Daisy* pushed her way steadily up the Wami. But progress was maddeningly slow, for the river wound like a snake, and they seemed to be beating back on their own tracks. In spite of its deceptive breadth, the water was only a few feet deep, and there were innumerable snags. Massive tree trunks brought down by tropical storms lay across the channel, hidden sandbanks or shelves of rock jarred the keel plates, and they continually encountered canoe loads of hostile Africans. The black warriors would not let them pass until the white men had bought their way with gifts of beads and cloth, and there were long delays while they chaffered and argued. By night they tied up at the tree-clad bank, sleeping uneasily amid the terrors of the dark and the bloodsucking swarms of mosquitoes.

After eight days the explorers had advanced only about seventy miles. First thing in the morning and last thing at night Mackay took soundings. Grimly he reported that the river was dropping two inches a day. He and the leader argued it out over supper.

"We can't go on," the engineer protested. "We've no chart to guide us, nothing to mark the sandbanks. If we run aground we're stuck, and the launch will be lost. So will we," he added. "We don't know where we are, and there's no hope of rescue."

"I know, I know," said Lieutenant Smith

wearily. "But my orders are. . . ." He slumped in his deck chair, his head in his hands.

"Sorry," he mumbled. "Afraid I'm in for a go of fever. I'll turn in now and try to sweat it out. Take another sounding at first light, then we'll decide if we must turn and run for it."

But it was Mackay who had to take the decision on his own. In the morning Smith was delirious with fever. There was only one thing to do, make for the coast as fast as possible. He gave sharp orders to get the engines going and to cast off. For the next few days he had to be not only engineer, but also navigator, steersman, cook and doctor. But he was sure that he had decided aright. Whatever the difficulties of the forest paths, it would be quicker to travel on foot to the interior than by water along the tortuous Wami. It was with a sigh of relief that at length he sighted the rolling breakers of the coast and felt the salt breeze blow through his sweat-stained clothes.

But the open sea brought them near to disaster. The rolling waves of the estuary broke over the launch and in a few minutes they were swamped. Fortunately the *Daisy* grounded on the sand and stuck fast. Mackay's first thought was to carry his sick companion ashore before night fell. He made him as comfortable as he could in a near-by African hut and returned to stand by his ship. In the velvet dark of midnight he was still at work, transferring the *Daisy's* cargo to an Arab dhow he had managed to hire. At last, cold, wet, hungry, and utterly exhausted, he stretched himself out on some bales of cloth in the dark hold of the dhow to sleep until dawn.

*　　*　　*

It was a sorry start to the missionary venture, but Mackay did not lose heart. The *Daisy* was a sturdy craft, and with the help of his crew he refloated her at high tide a day or two later. But one thing was clear. There was no waterway to the interior. The journey to Uganda would have to be through the forest, a step at a time.

The missionaries divided themselves into four caravans for the eight hundred mile trek to the Victoria Nyanza. Each party had several hundred African carriers with 70 lb. headloads of equipment for the prospective mission station on the shores of the Great Lake. No one knew how long the trek would take or how arduous it would be.

They were soon to learn. The leader of the pioneer caravan died on the way, and two of his companions were invalided back to the coast. Mackay himself went down with fever and dysentery and had to turn back. It was a miserable retreat. So weak had he become that he had to ride on the back of a donkey, jolting through the undergrowth one weary day after another. By night his men lit a fire and lay round him in a clearing they had hacked out in the forest. Food was hard to come by. The smoked leg of a wild boar or a few tiny African eggs served for supper. His only drugs were the usual tropical remedies of the time, ipecacuanha which made him vomit, and laudanum which eased the griping pain of dysentery but left his brain dazed and fuddled. But at last he reached the coast and the fresh air brought healing to his fever-racked body.

Orders came from London that he was to stay on the coast until after the rainy season. It was a blow to Mackay's eager spirit, but a further message gave him a task to do which made him forget all his disappointment. He was to cut a road through the forest from the coast town of Sadani to Mpwapwa, some 230 miles inland. Mpwapwa was to be an intermediate station on the long route to the Lake, and the highway would open up the country for the advance of the Gospel and peaceful trade into the heart of East Africa.

*　　*　　*

It was a herculean task. First Mackay had to find workmen and train them in the use of the strange tools of the Western world. From his base at Sadani he foraged here and there for labourers for his road gang, and on these scouting expeditions he had several encounters with slave caravans. Men there were in plenty, it seemed, and women and children, too, but they were not for his employ. They were being driven in chains to the Arab dhows, never to see their homes again. At first

Mackay made hot pursuit, attacking one Arab slaver after another. But there was little he could do for the moment against the evil trade. The local chiefs pretended to help him, but he soon discovered that they were secretly sending word of his movements to the slavers. He had to make up his mind that battle was not his business. For the time being there was one thing to do, and one thing only; the making of the road.

Not only the Arabs were the enemy. "The African giant Mukunguru, or remittent fever, has attacked me and thrown me down three or four times," he wrote. "I have had hard work to get strength again. But I am again well, thank God, and have become quite indifferent as to the sort of accommodation I get. I have slept in all sorts of places—a cow-byre, a sheep-cote, a straw hut no larger than a dog-kennel, a hen-house, and often in no house at all. So anything suits me, provided I get a spot tolerably clear of ants and mosquitoes. Of all the plagues of Egypt, none could have been worse than that of the black ants!"

Mackay's right hand man in the making of the road was Susi, whose name is immortal in African history. Susi had been David Livingstone's faithful "boy", one of the two who had borne the great explorer's body through danger to the coast and had accompanied it all the way to the last resting-place in Westminster Abbey. The old African had much to tell about Alexander Mackay's boyhood hero, and, since he knew the language of the local people, he made himself useful in collecting workmen and interpreting the white man's instructions to them.

So the road was begun. There were about seventy men in all, forty of them to work on the road, the rest to be donkey-boys, cooks and carriers of large quantities of axes, hatchets, picks, spades and saws. Every tool was new to them, and the engineer had patiently to demonstrate its use. Even the donkey's load of iron nails was strange, accustomed as they were to using twisted coco-nut fibre to join things together. Here, in turn, Mackay learned from his workmen, for his iron nails twisted and bent against the hard timber of the forest, and he found the coco-nut fibre a more useful material to work with. But the machine of wonder and delight was the grindstone on which the missionary nightly sharpened the cutting tools for a new day's work. As it whirled and sparked in the dark of the forest camp, the villagers crept out from behind the trees to exclaim with awe at the white man's magic.

*   *   *

Mile after weary mile they hacked their way, slashing at the undergrowth, hewing down the giant trees, levelling the raw track. The timber was trimmed and used to build bridges which would withstand the torrents of the rainy season. The men toiled with a will, keeping time to a monotonous chant:

"Oh, is not the white man very bad,
Cutting down the trees
To make a way for Englishmen to come?"

Passers-by gazed in astonishment at the wide clear way, and the tale of the "big road" lost nothing in the telling in their compounds at night. But the local chiefs were not pleased. They heard the song of the roadmen, and took alarm at the rumour that the English were coming to take possession of their country. One chief confronted Mackay at a newly-made bridge near his village and demanded payment for the trees cut down in his area. Mackay told him in turn that it was he who should pay. "My men have made a bridge for you which you and your people could not make," he said shortly. "When I am gone, chief, you will call it your bridge, and you will make everyone pay who passes over it!"

The next thing was to see how the first fifty miles or so would stand up to wheeled traffic. Mackay built bullock-wagons after the South African pattern and drove them, a score of bullocks to a cart, along the new road. That proved even harder work than engineering the highway! On Christmas Day, 1877, he rested for a little to scribble a letter home:

"You should see me every day with clothes

26

bespattered with mud, and hands black like a sweep's, catching the spokes of the wheel every now and then as they get into holes, and yelling at the top of my voice to the oxen, till the forest resounds again. So much yelling have I to do in the six hours we march per day, that when I get to camp I am always quite hoarse."

He had to be here, there, and everywhere, by the side of the wagons as the oxen floundered in the mud or tangled the traces or broke loose. It was a strange Christmas for the young Scot, far from his own kin. But it was something that "worked", and he was satisfied.

"Sitting on the ground in the bush by night, and writing in a hurry, by the aid of a dim ship's lantern, allows me to produce a most miserable scribble. I am, besides, all the while tormented with countless mosquitoes and other insects; while the hyenas are smelling the oxen and growling all about. I have my Winchester repeater lying by me, ready for any friendly visit from such denizens of the forest."

*　　*　　*

He had to battle not only against wild Nature, but also against the treachery of men. The further he advanced from the coast, the more he walked in the midst of danger. One day he was resting in a filthy African hut when a band of armed men on the war-path suddenly invaded the compound, demanding the tribute of an ox. Each wild figure was armed with a fistful of throwing spears and guarded himself with a huge hide shield painted white, red and blue. They charged forward with a blood-curdling yell, their spears upraised, while Mackay sat tense and still, not knowing whether the onset was an attack or a salute. To have reached for his rifle would have been to invite instant death. Then, in a moment, the warriors knelt in a semicircle in the dust facing him, and laid down their shields and weapons. It was peace! But he was not left entirely unmolested, for they went off with some of his scanty possessions.

His food store, too, was constantly being pilfered by thieves who took a special fancy to his stock of biscuits. For a time there was nothing to eat except thick corn porridge which tasted like a mixture of sawdust and ashes. Mackay learned to pray in earnest: "Give us this day our daily bread." Even drinking-water, filthy as it was, had to be carried from a distance. Breakfast and lunch, he noted ruefully in his diary, had to be run into one meal, and, since it was eaten in the evening, it was also supper. But even in the worst of times he recalled the psalm he used to sing in the village church in Scotland:

> "The lions young may hungry be,
>   And they may lack their food:
>   But they that truly seek the Lord
>   Shall not lack any good."

"That's true, anyhow," he said to himself. "I have never wanted any day yet, and feel sure I never will."

Every step forward brought evidence of the desolation wrought by the slave-traders. Mackay watched helplessly while Arab caravans swung by loaded with tons of ivory which had cost the lives of men, women and children. Each company of traders had a straggling line of naked children at its tail, their necks linked together by chains, as they were whipped onwards to the coast for sale to the highest bidder. It was the "open sore" of Africa of which David Livingstone had spoken, and there was only one cure: a highway for the Gospel and for peaceful, lawful trade. In the steps of Livingstone, Alexander Mackay was making such a way.

"This will certainly yet be a highway for the King Himself," he wrote, "and all that pass this way will come to know His name."

3

THE GREAT LAKE

WHILE Alexander Mackay was blazing a trail through the forest to Mpwapwa, his missionary companions had pushed on towards Lake Victoria Nyanza. But disaster overwhelmed them. One had already died on the way, and two had been invalided. Only half the original party was left to go forward. Within a week of reaching Victoria Nyanza the doctor of the company succumbed to fever, and his three friends dug a lonely grave by the shores of the Lake. Then they set sail across the unknown waters to the northern land of Uganda, the goal of the expedition.

Further tragic news came to Mackay as he toiled onwards through the bush. It was only a rumour at first, too dreadful to be believed without confirmation. Two Englishmen, the story ran, had been killed in a battle with an African tribe near the Lake. They had given shelter to an Arab trader who had offended the local king, Lkonge, on the island of Ukerewe near the southern end of the Lake. In the fighting all three had been slain.

The rumour proved only too true. The two Englishmen were Lieutenant Smith, leader of the expedition, and Mr. O'Neill, a builder missionary.

Only one of the advance party was now left, the Rev. C. T. Wilson, and he was at the court of Mutesa, king of Uganda.

Mackay resolved to push on as fast as he could to join Wilson. He was marching into danger. The Arab traders of the country had vowed vengeance on Lkonge and his people for the death of their countryman and the African king expected an attack also by an English army because the missionaries had been murdered in his territory. But evil as the crime was, Mackay knew that revenge would be no good. He sent a word to the now panic-stricken Lkonge that he was coming, but in peace.

"Tell him," he said, "that the followers of Jesus do not avenge wrongs, but forgive them."

Fever, however, delayed the long, lonely march towards the Lake. The rainy season had made the track a quagmire, and Mackay was constantly soaked through. Perforce he had to stop for days in the midst of the forest and dose himself against shivering bouts of malaria. He found now that he could not eat the coarse native porridge, so adulterated was it with sand and dirt. Day by day he had to mix a meal for himself, boiling the maize flour into a thin gruel, and sitting over the fire until it was ready.

*   *   *

It was not until June 1878 that he struggled

through to his first sight of the Lake which he had known by name for so many years. From his road camp he had walked two hundred and fifty miles through forest and swamp, making wide detours to avoid hostile tribes and thankfully seeking shelter with friendly ones. But the vast stretch of sparkling water which opened before his gaze made a new man of him.

"As eagerly as ever the ten thousand Greeks shouted '*Thalassa! Thalassa!*'[1] in the immortal Anabasis of Xenophon, did I gaze on the silvery sea and thank God that now I was near the Nyanza at last. For had I not been two years and more on the way from the coast, and now an end to miserable marching was come, at least for a time? Had no: my companions succumbed to the climate one by one, and even reinforcements failed? Now I was here alone to hold the fort till better days should dawn."

In a hut in the village of Kagei, on the southern shore of Lake Victoria Nyanza, he found what remained of the stores which the advance party had transported from Zanzibar. Everything was in a state of confusion. The ex-slaves who had acted as porters on the long trek had looted the stores of everything they coveted, and left the rest piled in untidy heaps on the mud floor. Dirt and rust and white ants had also wrought their havoc.

[1] "The sea! The sea!"

Mackay's heart sank as he gazed at what looked like a pile of useless junk. He picked his way among the stuff . . . boiler shells and books, cowries and candle moulds, papers and piston rods, steam pipes and stationery, printer's type and tent poles, jars of carbolic acid, cartridges and chloroform, saws and garden seeds, travelling trunks and toys, tins of bacon and bags of clothes, pumps and ploughs. His precious tools and engineering fittings seemed irretrievably ruined, here a cylinder there a crank-shaft or an eccentric.

Worse was to follow. An African led him to the beach where there was a mound covered with grass. It was the remains of the steam-launch *Daisy* which had been head-loaded in pieces all the way from the coast. Mackay silently pulled aside handfuls of grass and surveyed what was left of the trim little ship which had been his pride and joy. Not a plank was sound. Some had been shattered by the teeth of a hippopotamus, others were hopelessly warped by the tropical sun or turned to dust by white ants. It was a sight to make him weep in despair.

What was to be done? Work, and more work, was the only answer. Alexander Mackay was a Scot and an engineer, and with dour determination he set to, labouring to make the boat serviceable with whatever materials were still left in the hut. Ten days' hard work from dawn to dusk enabled him to take stock of his stores and to

33   c

estimate what could be achieved. Books and papers were put in boxes, and tools were painstakingly cleaned of rust and polished until they were once again fit for use. Best of all, the bits and pieces of the *Daisy's* engine were carefully salvaged and put together. It was a great day when the engine stood complete on the mud floor, every screw in its place and the boiler ready to be riveted.

Next he turned his attention to the hull of the launch. Crowds of chattering Africans gathered round to watch the strange white man who sprawled in the sand beside his "big canoe" while he hammered and chiselled at the shattered hulk. He used plates of copper and sheets of lead and zinc from his stores to cover the holes, and caulked the seams with wild cotton which grew along the shores of the lake. It was a miracle of improvisation. The naked black children gazed in wonder as Mackay set his lathe whirring or melted down the fat of an ox to turn out tall candles. Bits of iron and brass, nuts and screws and bolts, all were neatly fitted into place.

"White man come from heaven!" they declared. Surely no ordinary human could perform such marvels!

They wondered still more when Sunday came round and all work stopped for the day. "Why?" they asked, and Mackay gathered them about him as he took his Bible and explained that it was God's book, and told them about the day of rest. In the simplest words he related how God had come among men in Jesus Christ. It was the happiest time in the week for Mackay.

"More than ever I am longing for the day when the necessary rough work of pioneering will be done," he wrote in his diary, "and I can settle down to spend every day in teaching the little ones." As he wrote he dreamed of the time when he would have a daily school for these lovable African children and watch them grow in wisdom and understanding. One day there would be a training college from which African youths would go out to serve their own people as teachers, engineers, ministers. Meanwhile he was making a start, and as he looked at the children playing about his boat he saw hope for the future.

*   *   *

The local people came to believe that Mackay knew everything, and could do anything. The hunters brought in their old flint-lock guns for him to mend, the fishermen besought him to make them hooks. There were constant requests for medicine for every kind of sickness. Unless it was nasty to taste they had no use for it, so the missionary had to mix up bitter draughts to please them. But Mackay was unwilling to be their doctor, sad though he was to see them suffer. He knew his own lack of skill as well as African suspicion. They expected, for instance, to be made well at once after swallowing medicine. If a patient died of disease they were quick to blame Mackay for killing him with poison.

Uganda was still out of sight and out of reach far across the waters of Victoria Nyanza. But the island of Ukerewe was only two days' journey away, and Mackay was anxious to pay his promised visit to the king who had murdered his friends. He sent a message to Lkonge asking him to send a canoe with his own men to fetch him.

"Tell the king," he said to the messenger, "that if he is afraid to come to me, I am not afraid to go to him. I shall leave my rifle and revolver here and come alone, in peace."

A week later the canoe arrived with a deputation of Lkonge's picked warriors. Mackay's men at Kagei begged him not to ask them to go with him, for they were afraid. They were sure that he was going to his death. He himself knew the danger, but to outward appearance he was calm and unafraid. He left everything in order in the hut at Kagei in case he should not return. His only precaution was to take with him a supply of quinine in case of fever and some sulphate of zinc as an emetic. Lkonge was well known as a poisoner.

The visit, however, went well, for Lkonge was eager to explain what had happened in the massacre of the missionary party. It appeared that the Arab slave-traders had played him false, and that he had meant no harm to the Englishmen. Mackay told the king that he believed his story and that he would write it down and send the news to England. He warned him to have nothing more to do with the Arabs.

"If there is more fighting," he said, "the white soldiers will come with guns, and you will lose your houses and your life as well. But I do not come as a fighting man. Let me bring two of my white brothers to teach your people to read and write and to know the Word of God. Then, indeed, there will be peace between us."

Lkonge agreed, and as a seal of friendship a goat was slain between them, and they exchanged gifts. So the unarmed missionary won the day, and good-will banished strife and fear. After nine days Mackay returned to Kagei to be greeted by a dancing, shouting mob on the shore, acclaiming the return of their friend with wild joy.

*   *   *

Day followed tropical day as Alexander Mackay toiled to make the *Daisy* sound and watertight. More than two years had passed since he had set out from England, and he had not yet reached his goal. It was a lonely life, in spite of the throng of African villagers who had accepted him as their friend and teacher. There was no one who could do his work on the boat. Sometimes he wondered if he would ever leave Kagei. Would other missionaries in days to come find only a lonely grave beside

37

a mouldering launch, the sad remains of a venture which had begun with such high hopes? Dysentery, his old enemy, and fever again attacked him, leaving him listless and as weak as an infant.

But the day came when all such doubts were forgotten. One evening Mackay heard shouts from the beach. As he went down to the edge of the water he saw a canoe skimming towards him, its paddles flashing in the evening sun. For a moment he stood stock-still, unable to believe his eyes. The next, he was running wildly across the sand to greet the white man who stepped ashore from the dug-out. It was Wilson, the only other survivor of the pioneer party of missionaries. For months he had been alone at the court of the king of Uganda. Neither of them had known for certain that the other was alive. The last Wilson had heard of Mackay was that he was somewhere on the forest road, sick with fever.

All weariness and despondency were forgotten as the two men talked the night away. Mackay had endless questions to ask about Uganda and its king and the prospect of missionary work there. Wilson, in turn, heard about the making of the road and his friend's encounter with Lkonge. Mackay's strength was renewed to complete the *Daisy*. The launch was too frail to be propelled by the engine, so they would have to make do for the time being with paddles and sails. But at last, on August 23, 1878, they set out, their patched and makeshift ship heavily loaded with stores and engineering materials.

There was no chart of the Lake, and the *Daisy* was too frail to venture far from sight of the coast. There was danger from the countless rocks and islets and that meant keeping continual watch by day and anchoring by night. More formidable still were the sudden gales which sprang up and lashed the water into foaming waves. Many a time during the first few days Mackay longed for the company of the martyred Lieutenant Smith. He would have known how to set the sails and navigate with an eye to wind and weather.

Five days out, a storm burst on them without warning. In a short time the sky was dark with clouds and thunder rolled unceasingly. Giant waves began to break over the little launch while the paddlers sweated to keep her head into the weather. Then, in an instant, part of the bulwarks disappeared and the water flooded in. The crew panicked as they felt the ship sinking beneath them. There was nothing Mackay could do but let her drift ashore, praying that they might go aground before the waters completely over-whelmed them.

Once again the *Daisy* was a wreck, and it seemed as if all his toil had gone for nothing. Missionaries and crew waded back and forward from ship to shore salvaging their precious stores and laying them out to dry on the beach. The sun shone again in a clear sky, but the surf along the shore pounded the wreck unmercifully, tearing the side from the keel and breaking the stern away from the rest.

The castaways built a makeshift hut from spars and sails and once again Alexander Mackay went doggedly to work to repair the shattered *Daisy*. As he said himself, it was like cobbling a pair of shoes out of a pair of long boots. He cut eight feet out of the middle of the launch and brought bow and stern together, using the planks from the centre portion to patch the rest. It took eight strenuous weeks, and the result was a strange and stumpy little craft. But the *Daisy* was seaworthy once again, and the missionaries ventured on. On November 1, 1878 they came to Entebbe, the port of Uganda, and disembarked to march to the court of the king.

4

AT THE COURT OF THE KING

THE capital of King Mutesa was a city set on a hill. A broad highway led up the slope among giant huts thatched with grass. So regular were they that they looked for all the world like a row of heads neatly trimmed by a barber. The houses were enclosed by a woven fence of tiger-grass, with guards at every entrance to bar the way to any unauthorized visitor. The royal palace itself was spacious and imposing. Altogether it was the most tidy and civilized town that Mackay had seen since he first set foot in Africa.

In contrast to the plain, travel-stained clothes of the missionaries, the people of Uganda seemed to be dressed in the finest attire. They wore yellow cloaks of bark and turbans ornamented with seeds, beads and shells, while the courtiers of the king were girdled with leopard skins, a sign of their nobility. Page-boys darted here and there as if they bore tidings of the utmost importance, and the court musicians celebrated the missionaries' arrival with a martial roll on long hand-drums and the shrill fluting of reed pipes.

Mutesa himself was ill, and could not see them that day, but he sent a gift of meat as a sign of welcome. Two days later the summons came for the travellers to present themselves at the *baraza*, or royal court.

A double row of guards lined the way as they entered the palace, and the drums sounded again. King Mutesa was seated cross-legged on a mat, dressed in a white robe and long black coat embroidered all over with gold braid. His head was shaved at the sides, leaving a high ridge of woolly hair like a cockscomb in the centre. On every finger and every toe he wore rings of brass and copper. The king ordered stools to be brought in, and the missionaries sat and waited for his majesty to speak. For ten minutes there was silence, then he welcomed Alexander Mackay to his country, and graciously accepted the gifts he had brought.

Crowds of small boys followed the white men back to their hut after the royal interview. It was evident that King Mutesa had been impressed by the young Scots engineer, for that evening a lavish gift of ten fat oxen arrived and loads of coffee and honey. It was a good beginning, and in the days that followed Mutesa showed his favour by repeatedly sending for Mackay to talk with him through an interpreter.

*   *   *

The Scotsman soon learned that Mutesa was a proud man. It was best to listen and agree with him politely as far as that was possible. To the African king, Uganda was the centre of the whole world. He asked many questions about faraway England, and spoke about visiting that insignificant little country some day.

"When I go to England," he declared loftily, "I shall take greatness and glory with me, and shall bring greatness and glory back again. Everyone will say: 'Oh, Mutesa is coming!' and when I return: 'Oh, Mutesa is coming back again!'"

Mackay nodded gravely. "Just so, your majesty!" he said drily. He could not give the king the lavish flattery he was accustomed to from his courtiers, but at least he could keep the peace with him.

But on one matter Alexander Mackay was firm. When it came to any talk of the Christian message, he spoke plainly. It was God's will he had come to proclaim, not his own. At first the king was willing to listen to the Bible story. On Christmas Day, 1878, for example, a special service was held, which the king and all his chiefs attended in their finest clothes. Mackay read the story of the birth of Jesus from St. Luke's Gospel, and spoke simply of his Lord and His love for all men. A day or two later an Arab trader turned up with supplies of guns and cloth which he wished to exchange for slaves. The price offered was one piece of red cloth, one slave; one musket, two slaves. But this time, at least, the trader went away without success. Mackay's passionate pleading won the day with the king.

"What man can make the human body?" he declared. "Why should you sell it for a rag of cloth which any man can make in a day?"

First and foremost Mackay had come to Africa as an engineer. Right away he fitted up a machine shop and smithy, complete with forge, anvil, lathe, vice and grindstone. It became the wonder of the district, and chiefs, slaves and small boys alike crowded round to watch the marvels of the white man. They gazed in awe as Mackay blew the smithy fire to white heat with his cyclops bellows and hammered the malleable iron to his purpose. They scattered with cries of alarm as he cast the red-hot hoe or spade into the cooling bath where it sent up a hissing cloud of steam. Then they crept nearer again when he held it against the grindstone to make it sharp while the sparks flew about his head. This was the greatest mystery of all. What magic power made the wheels go round?

He went back to his boyhood love of printing, to teach the children to read. He had his printing-press with him, and an early task was to print off some large type sheets of simple words in Luganda, the native language. The African boys and girls were quick to learn, and to ask for more. Mackay and Wilson had first of all to act as translators, for no one had ever printed a word of Luganda before. But soon there were sheets of reading matter containing the Lord's Prayer, the Ten

Commandments, and parts of the Sermon on the Mount. One day, Mackay thought to himself, there would be a whole Bible. Meanwhile he must work patiently and work hard: " A mushroom growth produces nothing lasting, hence we must be patient; still, I have little doubt but that if we sow much we shall reap also much, and that the harder the toil so much greater will be the result."

*　　*　　*

The real difficulty was to find time for everything, so much claimed his attention. Mackay was a countryman by birth, and he was quick to note how fertile the land of Uganda was. The climate was like that of an English summer, and the earth produced the simple crops of the people with little toil on their part. The staple food was green plantains, very like bananas, and so easily grown that the farmers cut down the whole palm to get at the heavy bunches of fruit. The starchy plantains were roasted in the fire or pounded to a sticky paste for the evening meal. But in his mind's eye Mackay pictured the rich crops that the land could bear: cotton, coffee, corn, rice and tea. There was plentiful iron in the earth, too, and fine white clay. If only the country could be opened up and given access to the coast! Once again Mackay's thoughts turned to the making of a road, a highway on which all men might pass for peaceful trade, without fear of wild beast or cruel slaver.

All was not Paradise, however. In the hollows between the hills were swamps where the mosquitoes bred, bringing fever to white man and black alike. The tsetse fly, too, made impossible the keeping of cattle and the use of ox-wagons for transport. Pythons of fearsome size lurked among the tiger-grass, and herds of wild buffaloes invaded the plantain fields, trampling down the food supply. Even in the town there was danger from wild beasts. One night as he went to bed, Mackay heard the frantic bleating of a goat from the shed near by. He seized his lantern and rushed out. The goats seemed safe enough, but all his fowls were gone. A leopard had struck a gaping hole in the side of their hut and made off with his supper.

Man's cruelty to his fellow-man was sometimes worse than the pestilences of nature. Alexander Mackay was constantly being called on to act as doctor to warriors who had been seriously wounded in battle with neighbouring tribes. They never seemed to cease from slaughter. The outcome of a tribal battle was always the killing of scores of the enemy and the carrying off of their wives and children to be sold as slaves.

Witchcraft, too, haunted the land. One day when the missionary was sitting with the king, several witch-doctors appeared carrying bundles of grass dipped in blood as an offering for the protection of the palace against evil spirits. The king took them reverently and ordered them to be put at the threshold of the door. Mackay could not hold his peace.

"Listen to me, O king," he began. "Your country is a great country, and you alone of all the kings of Central Africa are willing to hear and obey the Word of the one, true God. But your people want you to serve other gods as well, and that cannot be."

He bent down to lift one of the charms from the threshold.

"What kind of god is this?" he asked. "Is not God in heaven far greater than these bunches of grass?"

Mutesa shrugged his shoulders. "It is our custom," he replied, and his courtiers murmured agreement. What right had the white man to interfere with the old ways?

"A foolish custom," said Mackay firmly. "Look at this grass! What difference is there between grass in the field and grass in the doorway? None! It is a mouthful for a cow, that is all!"

The king changed his ground. "It is an offering," he explained. "My medicine men have brought it in worship of the spirits."

But Mackay would have none of this. "The true God asks only one offering," he said, "the worship of our hearts. Remember the words I have printed for your children to learn: 'Thou shalt have no other gods before Me.'"

Again the king tried to change the subject.

47

"You came to my country to make things for me," he complained, "and now you make nothing."

"I cannot make everything with my two hands," was the reply, "while your two million subjects go about doing nothing. What I shall do is to teach your people what I know; then they will have the skill to do these things after I die. But first I must be true to God, and teach His ways."

At length the king gave way. To the amazement of his chiefs he allowed Mackay to gather up the bloodstained bunches of grass which lay about the doorway and burn them. From that time forth no fetish marked the threshold of the palace.

*　　*　　*

Work at the smithy began with the first light of day, as the engineer missionary made hoes and tools for the farmers of Uganda or repaired and sharpened their worn implements. The regular payment for the blacksmith's work was goats and plantains, which the missionaries were glad to get. Thus Mackay earned his daily bread by the sweat of his brow, and earned, too, the respect and trust of the African. Beside him in the machine shed were his pupils, cross-legged on the floor, spelling out their reading lessons from the sheets he had printed, and calling every now and then to the white man to explain a sentence to them.

As they advanced beyond the first simple lessons Mackay found that he had not enough type to supply the printing-press. There was only one thing to do, and that was to cut his own letters. It was slow, painstaking work, carving type from blocks of wood. A day's toil produced only ten letters. But his pupils increased in number as the reading lessons advanced, and some of them learned rapidly. There was no paper to spare for writing, so Mackay made do with native boards which he smoothed at his bench. They looked rather like the slates of the village children in Scotland, and a piece of charcoal served for pencil. Even the headmen began to take an interest in this strange new skill, and there were times when the shed was crowded with visitors, old and young alike spelling out their first letters or following with a finger the words of St. Matthew's Gospel.

On one of his visits to the court Mackay took the king a gift of a dozen sheets of large alphabets which he had printed from the home-made wooden type. Mutesa was so delighted that he himself supplied the missionary with paper to print more. Probably he had bought reams of paper in exchange for slaves. At least it could be put to the best use. Soon the mission press was turning out a simple book of prayers and lessons for Sunday worship.

The king's next command was that his chiefs and soldiers of the guard should attend school, lest they be outstripped in knowledge by mere children and

D

slaves. The printing-press could scarcely keep pace with the demand for reading matter. It was a happy day for the missionaries when they heard the people read the Bible in their own tongue and say the Lord's Prayer together at the Sunday service. They encouraged them to persevere by offering gifts of portions of Scripture to all who could read them. Thus, within a year of Mackay's arrival at the capital, the Word of God spread among the Baganda. But would it always be like this?

5

MUKASA THE WITCH

"SEE this, O king!"

Everyone in the court crowded as near as they dared to gaze at the large coloured chart that Mackay held up to view. Mutesa nodded wisely, unwilling to commit himself.

"It has the legs and arms of a man," he observed.

"It is a man," agreed the missionary. "It is you and me, under our skins." He traced the coloured lines with his finger. "These we call veins and arteries," he said. "They carry the blood to and from the heart all over the body." He placed his hand over his heart and motioned the king to do the same. "Feel how it beats!" he said. Then he showed the king how to feel his pulse and count the throb of the blood.

Mutesa smiled. "It is like one of your engines," he said. "It never tires!"

Mackay looked on the courtiers, African guards and Arab traders who were waiting to do business with the king. He chuckled to himself to see that they were all trying to find their pulse, following the royal example. He rolled up the physiology charts from which he had been explaining the marvels of the human body.

"It is very wonderful," Mutesa acknowledged. His hand clutched his breast again as if to make sure that his heart was still beating now that the lecture was over. Mackay looked round the court, and raised his voice a little.

"It is the body of a slave, too," he added. "He also is wonderfully made." And Mutesa nodded thoughtfully.

* * *

Mackay would have needed to be a walking encyclopaedia to satisfy the king. He could never guess what Mutesa would want to talk about next. No sooner had he got down to work in the smithy than he would be summoned to the court to face a kind of general knowledge examination. What size was the earth, the moon, the sun and stars? What made earthquakes happen? How did the electric telegraph work, and the railway? So it went on, almost every day, and always the king had further questions. The truth was that Mutesa had a restless, inquiring, intelligent mind, and he delighted in Mackay's practical knowledge. Here was a man who knew how things worked! Many a time the engineer blessed his hours of reading in the manse at Rhynie and at college in Edinburgh.

Not everyone at court was pleased by the favour Mutesa showed the missionary. The Arabs were strongly opposed to him, for he took every chance of condemning the slave-trade which brought them wealth, and he preached a religion which was alien to their Muslim faith. Sometimes Mutesa astutely set the Christian and the Muslims in argument against one another. Once, for example, when Mackay had been preaching against polygamy, the Arabs reported his words to the king, knowing well that he had many wives.

"How can a man get on with only one wife in his house?" demanded Mutesa. "Who will look after his children and his cattle and cook the food?"

"You can have servants, as we have in Europe," replied Mackay, "but the law of God is that a man should have only one wife."

The Arabs broke in to scoff at his words. "Polygamy has nothing to do with religion," they declared. Mackay turned on their spokesman.

"How many wives have you?" he asked.

"Four," said the man.

"Why not five?" asked the missionary.

There was no reply to this, for everyone knew that the Koran, the sacred book of the Muslims, forbade more than four wives. The Arab changed the subject.

"Religion is a thing of pure belief," he said. "It has nothing to do with manner of life."

"Very well," Mackay rejoined, "why then did you not join the chiefs and me in the food which the king sent to us just now?"

Once again the Arabs were baffled, for they knew that the Koran strictly laid down that certain foods were forbidden to them. Mutesa and the whole court laughed at them, and applauded the ready answers of the young Scot.

*   *   *

But it was difficult to know how much of the Gospel message the wily king was really listening to, and how much of his agreement was mere outward form. Some days he seemed humble and earnest in his questions about the will of God. Prayers were held Sunday by Sunday in a chapel at court, and there was perfect quiet while the people knelt for worship. One thing seemed to impress Mutesa above all else, and that was Mackay's constant appeal to the Bible as the Word of God. It had its effect.

"Isa [Jesus]—was there ever anyone like Him?" the king cried out as the missionary unfolded the story of the love of God.

But there were other days when the Scotsman's words seemed to fall on deaf ears. Mackay's task was not made any easier by the unexpected arrival at the royal court of a band of French Roman Catholic priests from Algiers, who made no secret of the fact that they opposed the teaching of the Protestants. The Frenchmen had brought with them just the kind of presents that appealed to Mutesa. He leaned forward with a covetous look on his dark face as they spread their gifts before him on the floor, while the chiefs of the royal household murmured their appreciation. There were five repeating rifles of the best European workmanship, a box of powder and shot, embroidered military suits, bright plumed helmets, officers' swords, mirrors, silver plate, and other costly items. These were royal gifts indeed!

From the first the Roman Catholics set themselves to undermine Mackay's influence with the king. Apart altogether from their religious outlook, there was little love lost between the French and the British at this time, particularly in their rivalry in Africa. The priests were seven in number, and for most of the time Mackay stood alone. His C.M.S. companions, Wilson, and some new recruits, were occupied elsewhere in missionary work.

Mutesa was astute enough to notice the tension between the Frenchmen and the Scot, and he played on it. One Sunday when prayers were over, Mackay began as usual to read the Scriptures. He had read only a verse or two when the king broke in and told one of his chiefs to ask the Frenchmen if they did not believe in Jesus Christ.

"Why don't they kneel down with us when we worship Him every Sabbath?" he demanded. "Don't they worship Jesus Christ?"

One of the priests rose to reply. "We do not kneel," he declared, "because if we did, it would mean that we were not Catholics, but false Protestants. We do not join in that religion, because it is not true. We do not know that book because it is a book of lies." He waved a hand disdainfully at the Scot. "They believe and teach only lies!"

Mutesa turned to Mackay for answer as the repeated word "lies" rang out. He in turn tried to explain why white men differed in their interpretation of the Christian faith. But it was too much for king and people. Mutesa shook his head in bewilderment.

"Every white man has a different religion," he muttered. "How can I know what is right?"

*   *   *

Mutesa might enjoy listening to Muslim, Catholic, Protestant arguing about their faith. But in matters of life and death the ancient superstitions of his fathers held him in thrall. For a long time the king had suffered from a disease that appeared to be incurable. Now his medicine men began to whisper that he would grow worse if he listened any more to the teaching of the white men. Mackay found that the king was less willing to see him. The name *lubare* was being constantly whispered about the court, and he learned that the *lubare* was a powerful "spirit" in the form of an old woman who lived by the Lake and who was greatly feared by the people of Uganda. She had the power, it was said, to heal the king of his sickness by a single word. On the other hand, if he listened any more to the white man's talk, she would bring further evil upon him for his neglect of the old customs.

A trial of strength began between Mackay the missionary and Mukasa the witch-woman in whom dwelt the spirit *lubare*. What could the foreign preacher do against the age-old beliefs of the country? Day after day he saw loads of plantains and gifts of cattle, hens and slaves being sent to the lakeside as appeasing offerings from the king. He could only bide his time and pray.

"May God grant me another occasion to teach His truth on this important question!" he wrote in his diary. " 'He that believeth shall not make haste.' His own time will be the best time. May I not fail to redeem it!"

His chance came at last. At a royal *baraza* Mackay sat in silence until the king had given judgment on various matters. Then he stepped forward and confronted his majesty, asking permission to speak.

The king inclined his head. "Say on!"

Mackay took a deep breath. "What is a *lubare*?" he asked boldly.

There was an outraged murmur among the courtiers. It was bad, very bad, to talk openly about the spirits! But the missionary paid no heed to their scowls. He waited for the king's reply.

Mutesa muttered that the *lubare* could hold converse with the departed spirits of his ancestors. Mukasa must be treated with reverence.

"There is no such spirit," declared Mackay. "People who say these things are liars, and the chief of them all is Mukasa. I come before you in the name of Almighty God, and I beg you to have no dealings with this *lubare*, no matter who tries to persuade you to do so."

Now the fat was in the fire! King Mutesa seemed to listen with respect, but soon he dismissed the *baraza* and Mackay could only pray that his words had made some impression. But a few days later one of his young pupils told him that three houses were being built for Mukasa in the king's inner court, and that the witch-woman was coming to stay there with her retinue of medicine men.

The missionary returned to the attack. He challenged the king directly. "Is it the king's pleasure that I should cease teaching the Word of God at court on Sundays?"

"No, not by any means!" was the immediate reply.

"Well, then," Mackay argued, "now that your majesty and your chiefs have decided to bring Mukasa to the court, it is impossible to mix the worship of God Almighty with the worship of a woman who is an enemy of God."

One of the chiefs interrupted to say that Mukasa was only coming with medicine to heal the king.

"Not so," replied the missionary. "Mukasa is a witch, and everyone knows that she claims to heal people by enchantment. Medicine is a good thing, and we all want the king to be cured, but it is witchcraft this woman is feared and famed for. She wants us to believe she is a god."

The king nodded his head at this. "What you say, Mackay, is perfectly true, and I know that all witchcraft is falsehood."

The missionary's heart warmed to the king, torn between the old ways and the new. But the courtiers were angry, and they redoubled their efforts to influence Mutesa. A day or two later a messenger summoned Mackay to court. This time there was a great deal of urgent talk from the royal counsellors, and as the missionary watched their dark, excited faces and caught their angry words, his heart sank. At last the king gave his verdict, amidst the delighted cries of the people.

"We will leave both the Arab's religion and the white man's religion and go back to the religion of our fathers!"

After these words Mutesa's attitude changed towards Mackay.

"Why did you come here at all?" he asked harshly. Mackay replied simply that he came to teach his people the Word of God.

"That is not what we want," said the king. "We want men to teach us to make powder and guns, and to work for us."

Mackay looked round the attentive court. "I have never refused to do any work you have asked

59

me to do," he said, "and there is scarcely a chief present for whom I have not toiled. Look at my hands!" He held up his hands, blackened and rough from his long hours at the forge and anvil.

The chiefs were bold now that the king was clearly won over to their side. "We want no more of your teaching!" they cried. "We want guns, and caps and powder. We want guns as many as the grass, so that we may conquer our enemies!"

It was a sad climax to more than two and a half years of Christian teaching. Before dawn the next morning Mackay was wakened by the sinister roll of hundreds of drums and the frenzied shouts of the women. It was the procession of Mukasa making her triumphant way to the royal palace. An orgy of beer drinking followed, while the court musicians sang and danced in honour of the *lubare*. But Mackay heard little of what was going on at court. He went quietly on with his work at the smithy, praying all the while that better days would dawn for Christ's kingdom in Uganda.

* * *

The following Sunday he kept away from the chapel at court and held a brief service of worship at his own house with his African servants. He learned later that a large number of people had gathered in the chapel as usual and that the king had sent messengers to find out if he were there. It was plain that Mutesa was a little ashamed of his performance the previous week, and still desired the friendship and teaching of the missionary. But he was gripped by the old ways of his people. Before the end of the year, however, Mackay heard that Mukasa the sorceress had gone back to the Lake with all her company. In spite of her magic charms and incantations she had failed to cure the king.

What would happen next, he wondered. He knew that Mutesa was a strong man, and intelligent far above the average. What a power for good he might be, since his word was law among two million people! But there was a dark streak of cruelty in him too, and pain made him as savage as a wild animal. As his disease grew worse, the king struck out in all directions, giving orders for the wanton slaughter of hundreds of innocent victims.

It was an African orgy at its most fearful. A reign of terror began in which no one knew who would be the next victim of Mutesa's lust for blood. The king sent out executioners on every road radiating from the capital to kill anyone they could find on the highway. Farming folk coming in from the hills with their head-loads of produce for market were seized and dragged into a compound, tied in forked sticks until dawn, and then slaughtered. They were accused of no crime, for none had been committed. Their only offence was that they had no friends among the powerful

61

chiefs of the court. It was the king's pleasure that so many be butchered every day. The executioners must do his will wherever they could find men, women or children to seize and slay.

A day came when one of the king's witch-doctors thought of another "cure". His majesty must give orders for human sacrifice to be offered on all the hills round about the capital. The executioners led their gangs of cut-throats out to every track to lie in wait for the peasants coming in from the plantations. One night Mackay heard a wild commotion outside his own house as five men were suddenly seized. He was powerless to intervene. On another track forty men and thirty women were taken before sunset. Some of Mackay's young scholars disappeared, never to be heard of again. Then came the day of the *kiwendo*, or great slaughter for which the wretched captives were being saved. The witch-doctors in hideous masks did their dreadful work. Some of the victims had their throats cut, but others were slowly tortured to death, being first blinded, then tied hand and foot, covered with dry reeds and firewood, and burned alive.

Mutesa had thrown off all pretence of being interested in Christian teaching. He refused to see Mackay. The only thing the missionary could do was to write a letter, begging the king to stop this terrible slaughter of his subjects.

"We are not the king or chiefs of Uganda," he

wrote. "We only pray your majesty not to allow these people, who have done no wrong, to be put to death. The great God has given a commandment in His Book: 'Thou shalt not kill,' and if this great wickedness is done, breaking God's law, He will be very angry with you, and will send His punishments. Besides this, killing so many people, fighting and robbing neighbouring countries, will make your country very weak. The king is king over people, and if the land has no inhabitants, what can the king reign over? The more inhabitants there are in a country, the stronger and richer the king becomes.

"We daily pray that God may give you His blessing in all things, and give you a wise heart, through Jesus Christ's sake."

In his diary Alexander Mackay put down his own stubborn faith: "The tide will turn. This I believe and know, because I trust in God."

6

NO SUCH WORD AS "IMPOSSIBLE!"

MUTESA had set his face against the missionary, and the people took their cue from the king. Mackay found it hard to buy food, for the Africans were afraid to show any favour to the white man so long as the king was displeased with him. There came a day when he was glad enough to take the glass from some pictures his father had sent him from Scotland. He silvered the glass and sold it as mirrors in the market-place to keep the wolf from the door.

But he was not going to leave Uganda! Alexander Mackay had all the granite determination of the Aberdonian, and he was going to stick it out, even in the midst of murder and witchcraft. He was sure that nothing could withstand the Gospel for long.

"The burning of a few straws will make a smoke," he wrote to his father, "and for a time the stars are invisible in the sky. But the flame dies out at length, and still clearly shines the morning star, the sign of the gospel of peace."

One thing, however, he must do, and that was replenish his supplies. The mission was utterly without food and barter goods, except for the scanty rations he could earn at the smithy. It was impossible to remain at the capital of Mutesa without materials for making gifts for the greedy king. Mackay made up his mind to make the long journey to the base-camp at Uyui, on the road from the coast, to bring up goods to his empty store-house and to replenish his machine-shop.

*   *   *

First he had to spend a week at the lakeside, begging one chief after another to give him canoes for the passage across the Nyanza. They tried to put him off with evasive excuses.

"It is the fishing season," said one. "All my canoes are needed."

"Your loads will be too heavy," grumbled another. "Besides, my paddlers have a quarrel with the people on the other shore. If they go with you unarmed, they will never return."

"If I don't go, there will be no more wonderful gifts for the king," said Mackay shortly. He knew well the real reason for their reluctance to help. "Then when the smithy fire is out, and the wheels no longer turn, what shall I say to Mutesa? Shall I say: 'O king, your chiefs would not help me with canoes. That is why I have no iron to repair your guns and type to print your books'?"

The men shifted uneasily. Mutesa might be angry with them, but perhaps the white man was right. His bright blue eyes stared at them, as clear as the Lake itself.

E

"Well?" he demanded. "How many canoes will you give me?"

He got his fleet of frail, tiny craft and set out on the voyage that was to take thirty days under the burning sun. Each morning the leading paddler rose in the prow of the canoe and held out a banana on the blade of his paddle and dropped it in the water as an offering to the spirits of the Lake. Every paddler had charms about his neck and arms as a protection against the hazards of the voyage.

The practical missionary had no time for such superstition. One day he bought a great and powerful charm and gathered his men about him to talk to them about the worthlessness of such idols.

"What is in this charm?" he demanded.

"It is *lubare*, a spirit-thing," was the awed reply.

"Will it burn?" asked Mackay.

"No, the *lubare* does not burn."

"This charm is mine, isn't it?" the missionary went on. They agreed that it was his, since he had bought it.

"Well then, I can do with it what I like?" The men nodded, wondering what was coming next.

"Very good," concluded Mackay, as he took out his pocket lens. He ordered one of the boys to gather some driftwood for a fire. Then, putting the magic charm on the top, he focused the rays of the sun on the bundle with his lens. In a few minutes the pile was ablaze, charm and all.

There was an awed silence among the paddlers. "Can your medicine men make fire from the sun as I have done?" asked Mackay. They shook their heads. This was magic indeed! Half of them backed away in horror at the white man's daring. The others expected the spirits to strike him dead on the spot. Mackay waited until the charm had been reduced to ashes.

"Now the devil is dead," he said, "and you all see that I have told you true, that there is no saving power in charms. God alone can save us."

*   *   *

It was several months before Mackay got his loads safely to Uganda. He quietly took up work again at the smithy, waiting to see whether Mutesa would smile or frown. He soon found that the king was more against him than ever. Two Arab traders whom he had never seen before in his life had arrived from the coast with the fantastic story that Mackay was a desperate murderer who had escaped from England. The truth was that some of the C.M.S. missionaries had intercepted the Arabs on their way to the coast with a company of slaves. They had decided that the road-maker was the ringleader of the Christians who interfered with their trade. They gave him no peace, stirring up the people to steal his goods, and constantly denouncing him before the king as a dangerous criminal.

"He will steal your land and your power and everything you possess," they insisted. Then they told a cunning tale to persuade Mutesa to have Mackay put to death.

"A certain king," the fable ran, "had a favourite cat, which was reported one day to have eaten all the eggs. The king, however, said: 'It is my cat; let it alone, it must eat.' Next day it was reported to have eaten the fowls. 'Leave it alone,' said the king; 'it is my favourite cat, it must eat.' After this it ate up the goats, then the cows, but still the king would not let the cat be touched. Next it ate up all the people, and the king's wives, then his children, and finally it ate up the king himself.

"Only one son of the king escaped by hiding himself. Meanwhile the cat grew and swelled up to a great size, having devoured so many things. At last the one prince who escaped succeeded in killing the cat. When he cut it open he found in it all the eggs, fowls, goats and cows, and the people and wives and the king's sons. But as he cut the cat open, the prince accidentally wounded in the leg one of his brother princes. This youth got out and demanded: 'What did you wound me for?'

" 'Did you not see,' said his brother, 'that I have been doing you a good turn in letting you out?' But he refused to be at peace, and tried to kill the prince who had let him out!

"The wonderful cat," said the Arabs, "is the

English, and the wounded prince who wished to kill his deliverer is Mackay. You, Mutesa, have conferred every benefit on him, but he means only to return you evil for good."

Hatred and lies did not make the Scot budge one inch. He remembered the rhyme they used to chant in his schooldays:

"Sticks and stones
May break your bones,
But names will never hurt you!"

He did not try to answer back, or to pay his enemies at court in their own coin. There was plenty of work to do, and he was happy to do it.

* * *

One of his jobs in these difficult days was to provide the mission with a proper water supply. Hitherto all water had had to be carried from a pool among the swamps some distance away. There was always danger that the chiefs might prevent his servants from drawing water, or attack them on the way. Here his training as an engineer came into play. He prospected the area all round the mission house, noting that under the red-sandy earth of the neighbourhood there was a layer of blue, potter's clay.

The people watched him curiously, and he heard them asking questions among themselves. He pointed to the spot. "Water!" he said impressively. "Dig down until three men could stand one on top of the other. There you will find water, and I shall bring it up for us to drink!"

A gang of men was set to work with pick and spade to dig a hole eight feet by four. When they got down too far to throw out the earth easily, Mackay set up a tripod of tree trunks with a rope and pulley and bucket to bring up the clay. After a week's work they found water, just where Mackay had predicted, at a depth of sixteen feet. Then he installed a battered pump which he had bought in London, and before long the water was rising, rising, and flowing strong and clear.

The Africans danced round in wild excitement. Never had they seen anything like this!

"*Mackay lubare! Mackay lubare dala!*" they cried. "Mackay is the great spirit! Truly he is the great spirit!"

The engineer hushed them. "There is only one great Spirit, that is God," he said. "I am only a man like yourselves." He would have no superstitious beliefs about the well. He carefully explained to each crowd of visitors how it worked. The pump, he told them, was like an elephant's trunk made of copper, which sucked up the water. But the Africans only half understood his patient explanations. To them it was magic.

"Oh, the white men, the white men, they can do everything!" they shouted. "Even the Arabs can only draw water in the swamp where we get it ourselves. But oh, oh, Mackay is clever, clever! Let us tell the king about this wonderful thing!"

Mackay smiled, and went on with his work. His next task was to put up a proper house for the other missionaries who were to join him at the capital. It was a building of European style, with panelled doors, window frames covered with wire gauze in place of glass, and, most wonderful to African eyes, a second storey reached by an outside staircase. His colleagues praised its comfort and coolness as though it were a palace. Even Mackay seemed pleased with his handiwork.

"Aye, it's no' bad!" he agreed. From a Scot that was praise.

He himself went on living in a native hut, making the excuse that he must be near his machinery, forge and tools. Thus he had begun, and thus he would continue to live in Uganda. But the mud house had its inconveniences, especially from the hordes of driver ants which continually invaded the place. Night after night they swarmed in their black battalions across the floor, in spite of the hot ashes which he spread to keep them at bay. It was the smell of printer's ink which attracted them, and as Mackay worked at the press the soldier ants spread over table and papers and missionary alike until he had to flee from their ferocity by running out of doors, tearing the creatures from his legs and arms where they clung and bit into his flesh. At other times there were snakes to contend with, snakes which slithered softly over the mud floor to pursue the rats which infested the store-room.

*   *   *

The years of patient toil and teaching brought their reward. One morning a youth named Sembera turned up at the smithy and held out to the missionary a rather grubby piece of paper. Alexander Mackay gave him a warm welcome, for Sembera had been one of his first pupils. Because he was a slave boy, he had had to leave the mission and go with his master to work in a distant village. But he had never forgotten the words of the Bible he had helped the white men to translate. Now he stood smiling as Mackay unfolded the letter he had brought.

It was written in Luganda with a pointed piece of spear-grass by way of pen, in ink made of soot and plantain-juice. It ran thus:

"Bwana Mackay, Sembera has come with compliments and to give you great news. Will you baptize him, because he believes the words of Jesus Christ?"

Nothing could have given Alexander Mackay greater joy than the news in that laboriously scrawled scrap of paper. The slave boy was the very first to be baptized, and he proudly took his teacher's name and became Sembera Mackay.

It was a red-letter day for the mission, the beginning of the Christian Church in Uganda.

When other missionaries came to the capital Alexander Mackay set out for the southern end of Lake Victoria Nyanza to build a boat to keep them in touch with their base at Kagei and to transport their supplies. The vessel had been brought out in sections by Bishop Hannington on his first visit to Africa, but it had to be dumped on the southern shore of the Lake until a skilled craftsman could put it together.

At Kagei he was glad to welcome a man after his own heart. George Wise was a tinsmith by trade, but he could turn his hand to almost anything. The two men scouted about for a suitable site for their "boat-building yard", as Mackay called it. They struck a snag in the attitude of the local people. The king was very much afraid of white men, and he did not want them in Urima, his lakeside territory. One of his complaints was that Mackay would "steal his face" [take his photograph] and send it to the coast for all the world to laugh at. Everything the missionary did roused suspicion. When he sat reading a book the people said he was divining mischief. When he wrote strange signs on white paper it was witchcraft.

The mission camp was at a lonely spot some fifty feet above the near-by Lake. Behind the camp was the primaeval forest, but in front of them was a magnificent view across a bay, with high hills on either side. To the young engineer it was a constant reminder of home, an African replica of a Scottish loch among the hills. But the papyrus reeds that fringed the Lake were the breeding-ground of myriads of mosquitoes which brought torment every evening when the sun went down. As soon as it was dusk the missionaries had to build smoky fires and crawl under their mosquito nets to escape being eaten alive.

* * *

Twelve miles away, at Msalala, they found the parts of the mission ship *Eleanor* which they were to put together. Mackay's heart sank to his boots when he surveyed the pile of planks and equipment from which he was supposed to construct a sea-worthy boat. Here was the ill-fated *Daisy* all over again. The missionary who had brought the equipment from the coast had left them carefully packed in a tent to protect them from sun and rain. But as soon as the white man had gone on his way, the chief of Msalala had made off with the tent and had scattered the planks here and there until they were warped and cracked by the sun.

The newcomer Wise gave one glance at the pile of twisted timber.

"We'll never make anything of that stuff," he said. "It's no use for anything but firewood."

He did not know the Scotsman. "Impossible"

74

was a word which Mackay would not allow. He ordered his men to drag the timber to the camp at Urima, beside the Lake. Then, in face of the enmity of the king, the menace of the mosquitoes, and the wretchedness of their materials, he went doggedly to work.

First, Mackay set up a makeshift smithy to forge bolts and straps for the keel joints. Timber was obtained from a few of the planks which were still usable and by sawing a giant tree into boards. George Wise was his right-hand man, buying ground-nuts and pounding them for oil to make paint, setting things in order, improvising materials. It took three months of feverish work, during which Mackay cut and shaped every plank and drove every nail. But at last the ship was caulked, launched, and rigged ready for the voyage.

It was good to be afloat in deep water again, with the *Eleanor* stored with meat, firewood, and bales and boxes of supplies from the coast. Good, too, to be out of reach of the terrible mosquitoes, and to know that the ship was well found for the voyage across the Lake. Mackay privately added the Luganda name *Mirembe* [Peace] to the English name *Eleanor*. He left the others at Msalala to set up a mission station there, and turned once more to the north. With a crew of African boys to help he did the voyage in the record time of four days, without sight or sound of storm. They reached the capital on December 21, in good time for Christmas.

That was the happiest Christmas Alexander Mackay ever knew in Africa. The *Eleanor Mirembe* was safely in harbour with ample stores, and there was now a link with the mission stations to the south of the Lake. For the time being there was peace at the court of the king. Best of all, a large company of youths had come forward for baptism. On the morning of Christmas day they gathered in the church to make confession of their new-found faith in *Isa Masiya* [Jesus Christ].

That night, under a sky full of stars, the missionaries held a Christmas party for their African friends. Two or three fat cows were killed for the feast, and a huge plum pudding was concocted. Every guest had a share of the *pudini*, as they called it. They ate until they could eat no more. Then, before they slept, white men and black alike joined in the hymns which told of the coming of *Isa* [Jesus] to earth, long, long ago.

7

TIME OF TERROR

"MASSA! Massa! Wake up!"

A hand clutched Mackay's shoulder and shook him awake. A frightened boy was shouting in his ear. "Very bad storm, Massa! Look!"

For a moment Mackay thought he was dreaming. The boat was almost motionless on the Lake. The water was the colour of lead, and still as a pond. Not a breath of wind stirred. Then, suddenly wide awake, he saw where the boy pointed. Across the sky ahead there was a line of cloud as black as midnight. A wall of rain was sweeping towards them like an express train. Half a league away the water was whipped to fury. The eerie moan of the approaching tempest grew to a roar as it raced down on them.

Mackay sprang to action.

"Get the sails down!" he yelled. "Quick! Stow everything, and hold on for your lives!"

He threw himself on the tiller. There was no hope of avoiding the storm or running before it. The boat was well out in the Lake, beyond sight of land. There was only one thing to do, keep her head into the gale and trust to God and the stout timbers of their vessel.

The two boys forrard brought the mainsail down with a run. A moment later the tropical rain broke over them, like a whip with a thousand lashes.

There was no time to stow sail and rigging in shipshape fashion. They crouched head down and held on for dear life.

It grew so dark that Mackay lost all sense of direction. The tiny craft plunged hither and thither, as if trying to tear herself away from his control. The hours seemed endless. His whole body ached as he struggled with the tiller. Then, as suddenly as it had come, the storm rolled away across the Lake, leaving a sky full of stars. But there was no sleep that night as they baled the ship and set the tangled ropes to rights and assessed the damage.

Daybreak was chill and misty, and the engineer and his crew were weary and shivering. They were thankful to make for the shore to light a fire and dry their wet clothes.

Then the sun shone to cheer them. "All right now, Massa," said his boy with a grin. "Storm very bad, but we get fine, fine ship!" They had cups of tea all round and launched out again in fair weather.

"I'm crossing the Lake as regularly as a ferry," Mackay wrote home. "You will have to excuse my atrocious writing. Half the time the boat is rolling like a whale, and I have to be always on watch to trim the sails and keep a true course. But somehow we always get through!"

*　　*　　*

He was the one vital link with the store-camp on the southern shore. But the longer he was away from the mission at the capital, the more work awaited his return. During the height of the wet season he came back to find that the tropical storms had battered his native hut to bits. He set his boys to cut grass for thatch, while he himself rebuilt the mud walls and made new huts for the donkey and goats and fowls.

A time of terror began when King Mutesa died. The new ruler, Mutesa's eighteen-year-old son, Mwanga, was weak and vain. He was haunted by distrust of the white men, and the Arabs played on his fears. The missionaries, they told him, would eat up his country and drive him out. Mwanga tried to scare the white men, playing with them as a cat plays with a mouse. Mackay got permission from the king to make one of his voyages across the Lake. But no sooner had he set out with his colleague, Ashe, and their crew than Mwanga sent a band of warriors, armed to the teeth, to ambush them on the road. The Africans were led by the Muslim Mujasi, captain of the king's soldiery and the fanatical enemy of the Christians.

The travellers were waylaid just as they reached

the Lake. There was panic among the porters who were carrying oars, sails and other things belonging to the boat. It looked like the moment of death.

Then Mackay took command. As the warriors danced about them brandishing guns and spears he spoke quietly to Ashe.

"Sit down by the side of the road and look unconcerned," he said.

The two men squatted cross-legged in the dust and looked calmly up at their foes. Mujasi was beside himself with fury.

"Get up!" he screamed. "You are commanded to go back! It is the king's order!"

"If you wish me to go back," replied Mackay, "you can carry me!"

They were hustled to their feet and dragged away, while their boys were seized and tied up. But Mujasi was nonplussed. If only they had struggled, or fought, he could have struck them down in open fight. After a little he allowed Mackay and Ashe to walk at their own pace, and when they came to the capital they were allowed to go home.

Mackay was as cool as if he had been crossing a street in Edinburgh. He marched to the chief judge to protest at their treatment. But Mujasi got in first with the story that they had tried to shoot him.

An ugly mob surrounded them as they left the

court, trying to tear the very clothes from their backs.

      ★   ★   ★

There was no peace for many a day. Their own lives had been spared, but their boys, who had done no wrong, had disappeared. It was several days before they heard what had become of them. Three of their most faithful Christian helpers at the printing-press had been cruelly tortured and put to death. Their arms were cut off, and they were then tied to a scaffolding with a slow fire under it. They were slowly burned to death while Mujasi and his men mocked them.

"Pray now," he jeered. "See if *Isa Masiya* [Jesus Christ] will come and rescue you!"

There was a strange outcome of this dark deed. One of the executioners was so impressed by the noble bearing of the dying boys that he came to Mackay, begging to be taught how to pray. In spite of terror and persecution, the Church grew. Less than six months after the death of these first Christian martyrs, there was a congregation of 173 people, and 35 took part in the Communion service. It was a living witness to the ancient truth: "The blood of the martyrs is the seed of the Church."

Ashe marvelled at Alexander Mackay's steadfast courage. He himself wanted to shake the dust of Uganda off his feet for ever.

"Not so," said the engineer. "There is work to

be done. It may be that we shall be killed. But we can leave behind us what they cannot destroy, the Word of God."

So, day after day they toiled at the printing-press, turning out hundreds of copies of texts of Scripture, hymns, prayers, and sheets of St. Matthew's Gospel in Luganda. Even in time of crisis Mackay refused to hurry his translation of the Gospel.

"Every sheet," he noted, "has to go through the hands of our best pupils again and again before they agree on it. They take a deep interest in the work in this way, and are proud to have their own Gospel." If the missionaries were driven out or murdered, their African converts would carry on the work.

They worked under the shadow of death. It was at this critical time that the news came that Bishop Hannington had been murdered as he entered Uganda.[1] The fact that Hannington had come into the country by the "back door" route through Masai territory, instead of directly from the coast, had inflamed Mwanga's suspicions of all white men. Truly they were trying to eat up his country!

Fear of what he had now done made the king more savage than ever. One of his most trusted headmen told him plainly that he had done wrong in killing the bishop. Mwanga had him

[1] Hannington's story is told in *Bishop Jim*, in this series.

put to death on the instant for daring to criticize the king. Then he sent for Mackay and Ashe to wring from them the names of his people who had told them of the massacre. For three hours they withstood the storming and bullying of the king and his courtiers. But they gave no information. Mwanga challenged England and all Europe to rescue them.

"What if I kill you?" he raged at Mackay. "What could Queeni do? What could she or all Europe do?"

Even Mackay came to believe that it would be best for the mission to withdraw for a time from Uganda. But how to escape? He thought of flight by night, but the Lake was twelve miles away, and there was little chance that they would make their way to the boat unobserved. Even there they could be pursued by fast war-canoes. The only hope was to leave the country one by one, as they had entered it. Obviously he himself would have to be the last to go, for he was the leader. But for the time being they had to endure the cruelty of the king, and wait for a lull in his rage. It was nine years since the Scots engineer had first arrived in Africa, seven since he had set foot in Uganda. There was no rest or respite, no hope of a peaceful furlough among his own folk in his native Scotland.

*   *   *

If Mwanga could not make Mackay and Ashe afraid, he could and did try to destroy their converts. The Christians who served at court were seized and hacked to pieces, their bodies being scattered about the roads as a dreadful warning to others. Marauding bands were sent out to catch and kill.

Mwanga next fell on the "readers", as they were called, the young pupils who had assisted Mackay with the translation and printing of the Word of God. Several of them were tortured and burned to death. One church member faced the king bravely when he was told he must die if he would not give up the new faith.

"Very well," he said. "I am a Christian. I am not afraid."

He was clubbed and thrown to the flames. Another was burned alive, and died calling on his executioners to believe in Jesus Christ. Thirty-two others were burned in one huge pyre.

But the Church did not die. Some of the Christians went into hiding for the time being, among them Sembera, and they sent notes to the missionaries to tell them that though scattered, they would remain faithful to their Lord. Now the full value of the printing-press could be seen. Mackay was helpless to plead with the king for his friends, but he could strengthen their faith by the printed word. He sent out a letter to the villages beyond the hills where the African Christians were in hiding. It was like an epistle from the early days of the Church. It ran thus:

"People of Jesus who are in Uganda, Our Friends:

"We, your friends and teachers write to you to send you words of cheer and comfort which we have taken from the Epistle of Peter the Apostle of Christ. In days of old Christians were hated, were hunted, were driven out, and were persecuted for Jesus' sake; and thus it is today.

"Our beloved brethren, do not deny our Lord Jesus, and He will not deny you on that great day when He shall come with glory. Remember the words of our Saviour, how He told His disciples not to fear men, who are only able to kill the body; but He bid them fear God . . . . . .

"Do not cease to pray exceedingly, and to pray for our brethren who are in affliction, and for those who do not know God. May God give you His Spirit and His blessing! May He deliver you out of all your afflictions! May He give you entrance to eternal life through Jesus Christ our Saviour!

"Farewell. We are the white men; we are your brethren indeed who have written to you."

On the other side of the printed page were the words of 1 Peter 4: 12-19.

*   *   *

The news of the death of Bishop Hannington and of the persecution of the Christians in Uganda eventually reached England. There were many who urged revenge. They sought the conquest of Central Africa by force of arms, and the over-throw of King Mwanga. But others took note of Bishop Hannington's last words, that he had purchased the road to Uganda with his life. It was not gunboats or rifles that would eventually conquer Africa, but the heroism of the Christian faith. When Ashe was at last allowed to leave Uganda he was able to tell the Church in England how loyally the Christians of the capital had witnessed to their faith. A letter from some of his African friends backed up his words:

"Mr. Ashe has told you how we are hunted, and burned in the fire, and beheaded, and called sorcerers, for the name of Jesus our Lord. And do you thank God who has granted to us to suffer at this time for the Gospel of Christ. . . . . .

"Finally, our friends, let your ears and eyes and hearts be open to this place where we are at Uganda. Now we are in tribulation at being left alone. Mr. Mackay the Arabs have driven away out of Uganda. Oh, friends, pity us in our cala-mity. . . . . ."

It was true that the Arabs had persuaded Mwanga to expel Alexander Mackay from his country. The miracle was that he was alive at all. The only news of him for many a month had come by letter.

"I have not the slightest desire to 'escape'," he

wrote, "if I can do a particle of good by staying. Your and my desire, and, I believe, the desire of all our friends, is that the Lord will open the way for the mission to be kept on, not abandoned. The *Eleanor* is in port, some twelve miles off, and possibly I might make a dash for it, but what then? Anything may happen at any moment, and it may be that I shall be led to adopt such a course but hitherto I believe I am doing right in quietly going on with my work. . ."

He tried to please Mwanga if he could, to show that there was no ill-will on his part. The king wanted a giant flagstaff for his palace. He supplied a gang of slaves to carry beams and logs for the scaffolding, under Mackay's directions. Then the huge tree which formed the staff was carefully pulled erect by ropes and pulleys. To the wonder and delight of thousands of watchers, when the scaffolding was taken away the flagstaff stood by itself! Mackay was not an engineer for nothing!

But the Arabs prevailed, and Mackay was told to go. One July day in 1887 he locked up the mission house, left four of his servants in charge, and made his way to the Lake. The *Eleanor* was lying on her side, leaking badly, and he had to spend some days at the old business of patching and repairing before she was ready for the voyage. Once again he set sail across the wide waters, a lone missionary, exiled, but still unafraid. He was never to visit Uganda again.

8

"THE BEST MISSIONARY
SINCE LIVINGSTONE"

ALEXANDER Mackay felt tongue-tied and shy. It was so strange to be among friends of his own race again in the busy, bustling camp on the southern shore of the Lake. Ashe was back, he was glad to see, eager to hear about his friend's adventures. But these newcomers, how young and fresh-faced they looked, straight from England! Mackay was a veteran by comparison, tanned and weather-beaten and wise in the ways of Africa.

At first light every morning they gathered for prayer before going off to their various duties. There was hard physical labour, clearing the ground for a new mission station, putting up buildings and breaking the soil. Mackay noticed that the new leader, Bishop Parker, had the makings of a first-class farmer.

The Scot learned, somewhat ruefully, that another boat was on the way from the coast in sections.

"The heavy end of building that will probably fall on this child!" he wrote, and he was right. This time it was to be a large steam-launch, capable of cruising constantly on the Lake. A long line of porters brought in the materials for the ship in head-loads—seventy loads in all, of rivets, fittings, rope, paint. The timber for hull and decks was to be hewn from the forest, some twenty miles away.

He spent an exhausting month in the height of the wet season with a gang of labourers felling trees, dressing them for sawing, and dragging them on a home-made wagon to the lakeside. Some of the logs weighed over a ton. It was every man to the ropes as they strained and pulled timber through the dripping undergrowth and over squelching mud. They were scarcely ever dry, for it was the rainiest month of the year, and the six-foot high dripping grass lashed them with chilly strokes as they pushed and pulled their way to the creek which was to be a slipway for the launch.

Once there, he had to build a boat-house. That meant turning out thousands of mud bricks. Mackay came down to inspect the work. All of a sudden he started forward.

"Headman!" he called. "See here! Who put these boxes on the ground?" He pointed to the loads that had come from the coast, crate upon crate.

The African shrugged. "The labourers put them for here," he said. "But I count them, Massa. No man thief any. They all there."

"I'm not talking about thieves," snapped the engineer. "Use your eyes!" He gave one of the boxes a mighty kick, and the whole thing fell to bits in a shower of dust, spilling rivets in all directions.

"Wai!" cried the headman. "White ants eat dat fine box." Hastily he called the men to lift the crates from the ground. Every one of them had been attacked. The tools and stores had to be repacked and put high off the earth.

"These little horrors are the plague of my life," Mackay said to Ashe. "Nearly as bad as the Arabs in Uganda!"

There were larger and fiercer foes also, for the forest was full of leopards which broke into the animal huts at night and made havoc among the sheep and goats. Mackay dug a trap near the compound and caught one of the snarling brutes. Its skin made a fine trophy to adorn his hut.

* * *

As always in Africa, it was a case of hasten slowly. There were so many other things Mackay wanted to get on with—a new translation into Luganda of St. John's Gospel, for example. Small wonder he wrote:

"Mission boats unfortunately do not grow of themselves; they have to be built, every inch of them. But," he added, "trees have been growing for ages, of the Lord's planting, and as we fell them, I like to think that He ordained them for this purpose."

Sorrow fell on their happy team when Bishop Parker and one of the other missionaries died suddenly of fever. Alexander Mackay read the burial service at the grave in the Swahili language so that their African boys might understand that their grief was comforted by hope in Christ Jesus.

The service took place in a storm of wind and rain. How many lives, he thought, had the conquest of Africa cost! His next letter home pleaded passionately for other volunteers to fill the ranks.

"Many are glad to *get* information from the heathen world; and the more the account bristles with dangers, and horrors, and murders, and massacres, the more spicy it is. If only our friends would busy themselves to *do* something for the mission field!"

His friend Ashe was taken ill and had to leave for the coast, and for months on end Alexander Mackay was alone again. A plague of smallpox broke out, ravaging the villages round about, and he had to stop all other work while he vaccinated hosts of people, old and young, against the disease.

Strange news came from Uganda. The country had rebelled against Mwanga, and the young king had had to flee to an island on the Lake. He sent a pathetic letter to Mackay asking for help.

"Do not remember bygone matters," it ran.

"Mr. Mackay, do help me! I have no strength, but if you are with me I shall be strong. Sir, do not imagine that if you restore Mwanga he will become bad again. If you find me become bad, then you may drive me from the throne, but I have given up my former ways, and I only wish now to follow your advice."

"Too late!" Mackay reflected, but he did what he could to get the king to safety. It was the Arabs who had seized control in the capital, and the Christians of Uganda were fleeing for their lives. Many of them came to join him, and he formed a kind of refugee camp for them. He set them to work on the mission farm to earn their food and clothing, and once again his reading classes were in full swing in the evenings. The day would come, he hoped, when they would be free to return to their own country as Christian teachers of their fellow-men.

*   *   *

One day an unexpected visitor appeared. It was the famous explorer, H. M. Stanley, the friend of Mackay's boyhood hero, David Livingstone. It never entered Mackay's head to think that Stanley was equally impressed by him, but he was, as his journal shows:

"When we were about half a mile off, a gentleman of small stature, with a rich brown beard and brown hair, dressed in white linen and a grey Tyrolese hat, advanced to meet us. . . . . .

"Talking together we entered the circle of tall poles within which the mission station was built. There were signs of labour, and constant un-wearying patience, sweating under a hot sun, a steadfast determination to do something to keep the mind employed, and never let idleness find them with folded hands.

"There was a big, solid workshop in the yard, filled with machinery and tools, a launch's boiler was being prepared by the blacksmiths, a big canoe was outside repairing; there were saw-pits and large logs of hard timber; there were great stacks of palisade poles; in a corner of an outer yard was a cattle-fold and a goat-pen, fowls by the score pecked at microscopic grains; and out of the European quarter there trooped a number of little boys and big boys, looking uncommonly sleek and happy; and quiet labourers came up to bid us, with hats off: 'Good morning!'

"A clever writer lately wrote a book about a man who spent much time in Africa, which from begin-ning to end is a long-drawn wail. It would have cured both writer and hero of all moping to have seen the manner of Mackay's life. He has no time to fret and groan and weep; and God knows, if ever a man had reason to be doleful and lonely and sad, Mackay had, when, after murdering his bishop, and burning his pupils, and strangling his converts, and clubbing to death his dark friends, Mwanga turned his eyes of death on him. And yet the little man met it with calm blue eyes that never winked.

"To see one man of this kind, working day after day for twelve years bravely, and without a syllable of complaint or a moan amid the 'wildernesses', and to hear him lead his little flock to show forth God's loving kindness in the morning and His faithfulness every night, is worth going a long journey for the moral courage and contentment that one derives from it."

Such was Stanley's verdict. "The best missionary since Livingstone," he concluded. Mackay himself claimed only that he liked "making things work".

*   *   *

The steam-launch grew beneath his skilled hands. He was like a boy again, the days all too short for the things he wanted to do. One day he called Sembera to come and see the ship. The African clapped his hands with delight.

"She is big past all!" he cried. "Now we will sail to my country and show my people that we are still their friends! This moon, next moon, sir? When she be ready?"

Alexander Mackay smiled at his friend's enthusiasm. "I don't know yet," he replied. "But I will tell you a secret, Sembera. Tomorrow we are going to rig up block and tackle to put in the engine. Come at first light, and you will see!"

But the next morning there was no sound from

the workshop when Sembera came at dawn. A cluster of workmen gathered, puzzled to find the furnace cold and the anvil idle. Sembera turned on his heel and ran to the mission hut. There lay Alexander Mackay in a raging fever.

For four days and nights his faithful boys watched by him while he tossed and turned in the delirium of malaria. Often he asked about the workshop, but he did not hear the answers. On February 8, 1890, he died, the faithful Sembera at his side at the end.

When they laid his body in its African grave, the little company of Uganda Christians sang: "All hail the power of Jesus' Name!" He was only forty-one, but he had filled his years in Africa to the full with love and service.